A PARENTS' HANDBOOK
Start with Love

A mindful guide to raising children with self-respect, resilience, and joy.

By Lương Hoàng Anh

Vancouver, July 2025

TABLE OF CONTENTS

ABOUT THE AUTHOR *Ms. Lương Hoàng Anh* 1

Acknowledgments 5

INTRODUCTION 7

CHAPTER I, PRENATAL EDUCATION THROUGH LOVE 10

  1. Nurturing the Baby with the Mother's Living Energy 10

  2. Don't Try to Teach, Just Be the Person You Want Your Child to Become 12

  3. A Mother's Emotions Are the Baby's First Programming 13

  4. The Root of Self-Respect Begins with Being Conceived in Love 14

  5. Begin by Returning Inward 15

  6. Practice Deep Breathing and Meditation, Cultivate Calm from Within 16

  7. Eat Wisely, Nurture Your Baby with Balanced Nutrition 17

8. Prepare Mentally, Let Go of Fear and Pressure 18

CHAPTER II – SELF-RESPECT STARTS WITH A SPOON 21

Eating: The First Lesson in Self-Respect 21

Spoon-Feeding vs. Self-Feeding: A Child's First Taste of Independence 22

A Mother's Regret: A Moment That Taught Me Everything 23

The Science Behind Self-Care in Early Childhood 23

Mealtime Is More Than Nourishment; It Teaches Awareness 24

Discipline Without Shouting or Force-Feeding . 25

Knowing When to Stop: The Power of Personal Limits 26

Family Meals: The First School of Human Values 26

Physical Self-Respect: The First Shield against Harm 27

A Note to Parents: Teaching through the Spoon Is Enough 28

The First Spoonful Reflects a Child's Future 28

CHAPTER III – RAISING FREE AND RESPONSIBLE CHILDREN 30

1. Freedom Is Not Doing Whatever You Want .. 30

2. Emotional Regulation Is the Start of Maturity 32

3. Honesty, From Thought to Action 34

4. Test Scores Don't Define Your Worth 35

5. Freedom Means Knowing What You Truly Want 36

A Real-Life Example: Ghini's Course Selection 38

6. There Is No Real Happiness in Living a False Life 40

7. Teach Your Child to Express Themselves with Honesty 42

8. When Your Child Falls – Don't Rush to Shield Them 44

9. Love Doesn't Mean Attachment 45

10. When Love Goes Wrong: Teach Them to Tell Real from Fake 46

11. Don't Give Your Heart to Someone Who Only Sees Your Value 48

12. A Good Man Doesn't Need to Be Wealthy .. 50

13. Marry Someone Truly Compatible, Not Just By Status 52

14. Teach Your Children to Be Responsible, Especially to Their Parents 53

15. Freedom Means Living Without Debt 55

CHAPTER IV – Falling Down to Learn to Stand .. 58

1. When Your Child Falls, Don't Rush to Lift Them 58

2. Help Children Learn from Failure, Not Fear It 59

3. True Growth Comes from Taking Responsibility 60

4. Give Your Child the Right to Be Wrong 61

5. Crying Isn't Weakness: Teach Children to Name Emotions 62

6. Help Your Child Stop Fearing Judgment 63

7. Parents Are Not Perfect, and Neither Are Children 64

CHAPTER V – Parenting with Wisdom and Love . 66

1. Parenting Is Not Sacrifice. It Is Growing Alongside Your Child 67

2. Heal Yourself Before Trying to Heal Your Child 68

3. Build Inner Strength Instead of Controlling Your Child 69

4. Teach with Words, Raise with Action 70

5. Love Doesn't Mean Doing Everything. It Means Empowering 71

6. Teach Love Through Example, Not Orders ... 72

CHAPTER VI – Choosing a Life Worth Living 76

1. A Child Is to Love, Not to Possess 76

2. Character Is More Precious Than Success 77

3. Don't Let Love Become a Debt 78

4. Compatibility Lies in Character, Not Wealth . 79

5. Choose Work That Makes You Proud, Not Others Happy 80

6. A Debt-Free Life Is Light and Noble 80

Conclusion 82

ABOUT THE AUTHOR

MS. LƯƠNG HOÀNG ANH

Work Experience

2001–Present

- **Founder & CEO**, *Stella Ivy Cosmetics Canada Inc.* – www.glacyo.com
- **Member**, City of Vancouver Disaster Assistance Team
- **Donor & Director**, Vietnamese Professional Association of BC (VPABC) Scholarship Foundation
- **Donor**, Ho Chi Minh City Fund for Educational Development

2013

- **Founder & Managing Director**, *Hoang Kim Gia Company* (Corporate Advisory Services)

2006

- **Founder & CEO**, *Creative Young Talent International School*

2002

- **Founder & Chairwoman**, *Stella Ivy Cosmetic* (Exclusive Distributor of ORIFLAME in Vietnam)

2001

- **Founder & Chairwoman**, *LUX Vietnam* (now LUX HOUSE, Exclusive Distributor of VORWERK Group in Vietnam)
- **Founder & Managing Director**, *Idea Development Company* (Project Financing & Brand Equity Services)

  - **Key projects included:**

    - Park Hyatt Saigon – Project Financing
    - Franco Vietnam Hospital, Ho Chi Minh City – Project Financing
    - Atlas Copco Vietnam – Brand Management & Bidding Strategy
    - Asia Commercial Bank (ACB) – Setup of VIP Service Center & Structured Products

Note: Idea Development Company was closed in 2012

1999–2001

- **Investment Officer & PR**, *World Bank – IFC/MPDF*

- **Projects as Project Leader:**
    - Establishment of ACB Securities Company
    - Capacity building for various SMEs (e.g., TCT Furniture, JOTON Paint, LE HOA Paper, VILUBE Fuel)
    - Training programs for the Vietnam State Securities Commission
    - Organised press conference for Dr. James Wolfensohn, World Bank Chairman, during his visit to Vietnam (2000)

1996–1999

- **Treasurer, Institutional Banker & PR**, *Standard Chartered Bank*

1994–1996

- **Reporter & Sub-Editor**, *Saigon Times Daily – Online Division*

1993–1994

- **Secretary & PR**, *TEXTIMEX (now VINATEX), Investment Department*

1989–1993

- While studying at university, worked part-time as an interpreter for the Italian Trade Commission, Swedish Consulate, and EuroCham.

Education & Certifications

- **B.A., Teacher of Foreign Language**, Educational University of Ho Chi Minh City
- **B.A., Finance & Banking**, Economic University of Ho Chi Minh City
- **Master of International Accounting**, Swinburne University, Australia
- **Professional Journalism Certificate**, Press Association of Ho Chi Minh City
- **Certificate in Securities Analysis and Investment**, State Securities Commission of Vietnam

- **Certificate in Investment Project Analysis**, IFC / World Bank

Languages

- Vietnamese, English, Chinese

Academic Distinction

- Selective student at Marie Curie High School (1987–1989), entrance exam score: 33/40

ACKNOWLEDGMENTS

Thank you to the maternal grandparents of Lu, Li, and Ghini for your endless love and steadfast presence in their lives.

Thank you to my beloved children — Lu, Li, and Ghini — for your kindness, hard work, understanding, and the deep love you show one another. You have stood by your mother through every challenge. You are the greatest love of my life.

Heartfelt thanks to my virtual assistant, Nguyệt Yên, for your thoughtful editing and dedicated translation of this book into English.

INTRODUCTION

This is not a book about parenting theories. It isn't a manual for raising successful, talented, or famous children.

This is a real-life journey. It is the story of a single mother raising three children, alone, from pregnancy onward. A story of being both mother and father. Of making mistakes, learning as I went, crying, and growing alongside my children.

Each page holds a lesson drawn from lived experience. These are reflections born from missteps and meaningful moments, times when I saw my children grow through love and through the self-respect they nurtured for themselves. I've written this as if I were sending a letter to my younger self: a woman who was confused, but always trying to do what felt right for her child.

I was born into an educated family deeply rooted in the Confucian tradition. There was an expectation that I would become a "red seed," someone who would bring pride and distinction to the family. I fulfilled those expectations, at least at first, earning degrees in Education and Finance, and later a Master's in

International Accounting. I worked as an investment officer at the IFC/World Bank, surrounded by prestigious titles and promising opportunities.

At the height of that career, and with many suitors around me, I chose something entirely different. I stepped away from it all to become a single mother. I was pregnant with twin daughters, Lu and Li, and I decided without ever getting married.

In Vietnam at that time, an unmarried woman having children was considered scandalous. Even more unsettling to some was the idea of a woman who could build and control her own life, without needing a man. To protect my peace and avoid public scrutiny, I kept the pregnancy a secret until my fourth month. Then, I moved into a private maternity hospital, the best in Ho Chi Minh City, and stayed there quietly until I gave birth. No one saw me pregnant. It was a lonely chapter, yes, but also a peaceful and deeply fulfilling one.

I believe children don't need perfect parents.

They need adults who love wisely. Those who are willing to grow themselves. Who knows when to step back? Who teach not just through words, but by how they live their everyday lives.

If you're a parent who has made mistakes and still wants to grow,

If you believe raising a child is also a path of personal transformation, then this book is for you.

CHAPTER I
PRENATAL EDUCATION THROUGH LOVE

The moment I learned, I was pregnant, I began to live differently.

Not because someone told me to, but because of a sacred instinct, an awareness that every emotion, thought, action, even my food and my breath, would plant seeds in my child's future.

Each moment a mother lives is a message to the womb.

That is the true beginning of education.

1. Nurturing the Baby with the Mother's Living Energy

To me, prenatal education was never about playing Mozart or practicing yoga to make the baby "smarter."

It was about living each day with intention, knowing that even an unborn child absorbs every vibration from the mother.

The womb is the child's first environment.

And the mother's state of mind becomes the baby's first world.

The fetus is not just a cluster of cells; it is a living being, deeply sensitive, soaking up the mother's emotions like a sponge.

When a mother feels joy and presence, that energy becomes a silent nutrient that feeds the baby's soul.

But when she carries fear, sorrow, bitterness, or resentment, those emotions can become "pre-verbal trauma." These wounds have no words but can remain imprinted in the child's being.

This is why, throughout pregnancy, I chose to live simply and peacefully.

I avoided drama, disturbing news, and people who spoke with cruelty or constant complaint.

I cared for my body and mind as if they were sacred soil, growing something precious.

I never tried to be a perfect mother.

I only tried to live kindly with myself, because I believed that was the best way to mother my child.

When a mother learns to love herself, her baby begins learning self-love from the womb.

2. Don't Try to Teach, Just Be the Person You Want Your Child to Become

A baby does not learn from words.

A baby learns from your energy, from how you see the world, how you breathe through frustration, how you forgive, and how you live in honesty with yourself.

And this learning doesn't begin when the child speaks.

It begins in the womb.

Prenatal education is not a technique. It is a way of living.

You don't need to become a teacher.

Just live a life of integrity, and you will already be your child's first and best lesson.

I once wrote:

"Prenatal education is a journey of the mother nurturing herself with love, mindfulness, and wisdom.

Taking care of the baby begins by taking care of yourself."

And I still believe that today.

3. A Mother's Emotions Are the Baby's First Programming

Modern neuroscience confirms what mothers have long felt.

The fetus responds to the mother's heartbeat, brainwaves, and hormonal shifts.

When she is stressed, her body releases cortisol and adrenaline, chemicals that can affect the baby's brain development and immune system.

When she is happy, oxytocin and serotonin create a feeling of safety, warmth, and peace in the womb.

"Before you could speak, my child, you already felt.

So I learned to live peacefully, so you could grow in warmth before your first breath."

4. The Root of Self-Respect Begins with Being Conceived in Love

A child who is welcomed into the world with unconditional love begins life with a strong sense of self-worth.

They know they were cherished.

They understand, even before memory, that they were not a mistake.

Self-respect cannot be taught later.

It must be sown from the very beginning, from the mother's heart.

That's why, during each of my pregnancies, no matter how hard it became, I never said,

"Because of you, I suffered."

I never wanted my child to feel like a burden.

They came to me as a blessing, and I was always grateful.

5. Begin by Returning Inward

I don't wish to turn prenatal care into a spiritual routine that creates pressure for mothers.

Quite the opposite.

To every expecting mother, I say: live gently and honestly.

Take time to listen inward. Forgive yourself.

Cherish the small joys. Let go of expectations that do not serve you.

Because when the mother is calm, the child will grow calm.

A child raised in peace and love will be more resilient than any child taught by technique alone.

6. Practice Deep Breathing and Meditation, Cultivate Calm from Within

One of the simplest and most powerful ways to nurture your baby with love is through daily breathing and meditation.

Breath is the bridge between body and mind.

When a mother breathes slowly and deeply, her parasympathetic nervous system becomes active. This calms her emotions, reduces stress, and transmits peace directly to the baby.

Each morning or evening, I would set aside 30 minutes.

I inhaled deeply through the nose, exhaled slowly through the mouth, and allowed my shoulders and mind to relax.

No phone. No news. Just birdsong, rustling leaves, and breath, cleansing my thoughts like a gentle rain.

At night, I would sit quietly on my bed, eyes closed and hands resting on my belly, simply listening.

Listening to my breath.

Listening for the tiny heartbeat within.

Sometimes, the baby would move, as if whispering back.

You don't need to be a meditation expert.

Even ten quiet minutes a day, spent simply being present with yourself and your baby, is a sacred gift.

7. Eat Wisely, Nurture Your Baby with Balanced Nutrition

Pregnancy is not about "eating for two."

It's about eating mindfully, with awareness, balance, and love.

Throughout all three pregnancies, I followed a few core practices:

- Eat five to six small meals daily to stabilize energy and reduce discomfort.
- Choose whole, natural foods: leafy greens, whole grains, fresh fruits, deep-sea fish, eggs, plant-based milk, nuts, seeds, and legumes.

- Avoid processed foods such as soft drinks, instant noodles, canned items, and sugary snacks, as they often contain harmful additives.
- Drink at least two liters of water per day, this includes plain water, fresh coconut water, or unsweetened natural juices.
- Limit sugar and fast carbs. Instead of white rice or bread, I used brown rice, oats, or sweet potatoes to better support the baby's brain and immune system.
- Avoid caffeine and only take supplements prescribed by a trusted doctor.

Eating with love is another way to say:

"I care about your future, and I'm nourishing it with every bite."

8. Prepare Mentally, Let Go of Fear and Pressure

Motherhood often begins with worry.

I remember lying awake many nights wondering:

"Will my baby be healthy?"

"Am I good enough to be a mother?"

"What if I can't give my child happiness?"

But over time, I came to see things differently.

Children don't need flawless parents.

They need parents who are willing to grow, who admit mistakes, and who walk beside them with love and courage.

Here are a few beliefs I embraced to protect my peace:

- Let go of comparison. Every mother has her own path.
- Be kind on tired days. Even saying, "I'm tired today, but I'm here with you," carries love.
- Say no to outside pressure. I stopped watching toxic news and chose to read books that nourished my spirit.

Most of all, I stopped viewing my child as a project that needed to succeed.

Instead, I began to see them as souls who came to grow with me, so we could both learn how to become better, more compassionate humans.

CHAPTER II
SELF-RESPECT STARTS WITH A SPOON

"Self-respect is not something to be taught later.

It is a seed that must be planted the moment your child learns to hold their first spoon."

Eating: The First Lesson in Self-Respect

It's not reading, speaking, or walking.

The very first life lesson is learning how to eat.

When I taught my children to eat, I didn't focus only on satisfying hunger.

I wanted them to understand:

- You don't rely on others for what you can do yourself.
- You respect your own body.
- You avoid placing unnecessary burdens on others when you're capable.

At one year old, I encouraged my child to hold a spoon and eat on their own. No spoon-feeding.

Friends and relatives were surprised, some even critical:

"Why make it so hard? Just feed the baby and get it over with."

But I saw it differently.

There is nothing sadder than a child who grows up not knowing how to care for themselves, even in something as basic as eating.

Spoon-Feeding vs. Self-Feeding: A Child's First Taste of Independence

When a child learns to feed themselves, they begin to trust in their own ability.

Spilled food, trembling hands, messy clothes, these aren't failures.

They're signs of growth, the early stages of discovering personal limits and learning how to move past them.

A Mother's Regret: A Moment That Taught Me Everything

When my daughter Lu was three, she vomited on the floor after a meal.

In a moment of panic, I instinctively pushed her away, afraid of the mess.

But then I saw her eyes, frightened, sad, confused.

That moment haunted me for years.

Because nothing is more "unclean" than turning away from your child when they're most vulnerable, when they need your comfort, not your fear.

The Science Behind Self-Care in Early Childhood

Early childhood education experts like Maria Montessori have shown that:

"Every self-care skill learned in the early years is not just a physical task; it is a foundation for building self-respect."

When a child learns to eat, dress, or wash independently, they begin to believe:

"I matter. I can take care of myself."

That quiet belief becomes a core of self-worth that doesn't rely on praise or external achievement.

It stays with them for life.

Mealtime Is More Than Nourishment; It Teaches Awareness

I never let my children eat while watching cartoons.

Because I wanted them to understand that eating is a mindful ritual, not a distracted routine.

They learned to:

- Eat with gratitude
- Stop when they are full
- Eat neatly, showing respect for the food and the people at the table

Mealtime introduced them to:

- Limits
- Self-regulation
- Social behavior

Discipline Without Shouting or Force-Feeding

Children will have days when they don't want to eat.

They'll spill food, play with their meals, or eat slowly.

I never yelled. I never forced them to eat.

Because I knew, force teaches fear, not self-respect.

When adults get angry at the table, children don't learn nutrition.

They learn to associate food with stress and control.

And slowly, meals become a battleground instead of a time for bonding.

Knowing When to Stop: The Power of Personal Limits

A child who can't stop eating when they're full, or who needs someone else to say "finish your food", may grow up relying on others for decisions.

I taught my children to listen to their bodies.

"If you're full, you have the right to put down the spoon.

But say it clearly and respectfully."

Learning when to stop is a foundational life skill.

It applies not just to food, but to spending, relationships, and emotional boundaries.

Family Meals: The First School of Human Values

I always insisted on shared mealtimes.

Everyone sat down together. No phones. No toys.

To me, the dinner table was never just about eating. It was a space where we:

- Learned to listen
- Waited for one another
- Apologized when we made mistakes

Where there's no shared meal, there's often no meaningful conversation.

When a child eats only in front of a screen, it becomes harder to teach gratitude and presence.

Physical Self-Respect: The First Shield against Harm

One lesson I've learned is this:

A child who respects their own body from a young age is more likely to protect it later.

It starts with something simple:

- Not allowing others to feed them once they can eat alone
- Not being forced to eat things in a harsh or disrespectful way

These small acts affirm:

"This is my body. And it deserves respect."

That early sense of ownership becomes a shield against manipulation, abuse, and emotional dependency.

A Note to Parents: Teaching through the Spoon Is Enough

We don't need to lecture our children about self-discipline, honor, or independence.

We just need to teach them through the spoon:

- How to hold it
- How to pick it up when it falls
- How to eat with care
- How to stop when it's time

These small actions, repeated with love each day, are the roots of a strong character.

The First Spoonful Reflects a Child's Future

Children who grow up able to care for themselves, who eat with awareness and self-respect, will naturally develop:

- Confidence in thought
- Discipline in behavior
- Clarity in personal boundaries

"You don't need to speak every language, my child, but you must know how to listen to your own body.

You don't have to be a genius, but you must know how to care for yourself before you care for anyone else."

That is what I taught my children, every day, starting with the very first spoonful.

CHAPTER III
RAISING FREE AND RESPONSIBLE CHILDREN

1. Freedom Is Not Doing Whatever You Want

I often tell my children:

"Freedom doesn't mean doing whatever you like.

Freedom means knowing what you want and taking responsibility for it."

That's a hard lesson to learn.

Teenagers sometimes mistake rebellion for freedom.

They resist rules but often lose their way when boundaries disappear.

I've seen many young people demand the right to make their own choices, yet blame others when things go wrong.

But as children grow, parents can no longer shield them.

If they are old enough to make choices, they must also be ready to accept the consequences.

That's why I teach my children to think through the outcomes of their actions.

Not out of fear, but with responsibility.

True freedom isn't about doing anything you want.

It's about owning your choices and whatever follows.

I don't discipline with anger.

I ask questions. I listen. I help them reflect and self-correct.

Through simple, steady conversations, I've watched them grow.

They stop reacting impulsively. They begin to pause and think.

I believe freedom and discipline are not opposites.

They are two sides of inner strength.

2. Emotional Regulation Is the Start of Maturity

Adolescence brings emotional storms, but not all teenagers express them with outbursts or rebellion.

My daughters, for example, have always been calm.

They've never yelled or argued with me.

When they disagree, they stay quiet, reflect, and wait for the right time to speak with clarity.

Even my youngest son, spoiled and sometimes sassy, has never been disrespectful.

That tells me one thing:

My children have learned to manage their emotions and respect others, even in disagreement.

But calmness outside doesn't always mean peace inside.

As a mother, I know they may still feel sadness or confusion, even if they don't show it.

So I don't force them to talk.

I don't interrogate.

I just repeat one message, over and over again:

"If there's ever anything you need help with, just let me know.

Whatever you want to do, I'll always support you."

No pressure. No hovering.

Just quiet presence and trust, so they know:

I don't interfere in their lives, but I'm always here.

They share, not because they're forced to, but because they know that, in this world,

Mom is the safest place to be themselves.

3. Honesty, From Thought to Action

Teenagers often face choices between truth and loyalty, between doing what's right and protecting a friendship.

For example, when a child sees a friend do something wrong, they may stay silent, yet feel conflicted inside.

What matters in these moments isn't that parents demand honesty.

We must help children understand their feelings.

Guilt, confusion, shame, these are not signs of weakness.

They are signs of a living conscience.

I tell my children:

"Honesty doesn't mean saying everything out loud.

It means not betraying your sense of right and wrong.

Sometimes, silence can also be an honest choice, if you understand why you choose it."

Children need support to see that honesty is not about exposing others.

It's about being true to themselves.

It's about consistency between thought, speech, and action.

4. Test Scores Don't Define Your Worth

Many loving parents become overly focused on grades.

Exams turn into pressure points.

But high scores don't guarantee character.

They don't teach resilience or help children find what they truly love.

I never pressured my children about marks.

Instead of asking, "What score did you get?" I ask:

- Did you understand the lesson?
- What part did you enjoy most?
- Can you connect this subject to real life?

I encourage them to learn for understanding, for growth, for themselves.

Not to compete.

A child may never be first in class, but still grow into someone thoughtful, compassionate, and responsible.

And to me, that is true success.

5. Freedom Means Knowing What You Truly Want

Over the years, I've realized:

The deepest goal of education is not obedience.

It is self-knowledge.

The hardest part of that journey is not defiance, it's confusion.

Most children don't truly know what they want.

They are surrounded by noise: family expectations, peer pressure, social media, influencers.

If they lack inner clarity, they begin to mistake others' dreams for their own.

And when you live by borrowed desires, you feel lost.

That's why I teach my children:

"Freedom isn't doing whatever you want.

It's knowing what you want, and taking full responsibility for it."

No one can map your life for you.

But I can help you:

- Listen to your inner voice
- Tell the difference between true desire and temporary emotion
- Question both yourself and the world around you

I don't want them to chase society's idea of success.

I want them to live with intention, with the strength to make their own choices, and own the outcomes.

A child who knows what they want may not always be the best.

But they are the hardest to manipulate.

A Real-Life Example: Ghini's Course Selection

One day, when my son Ghini was in 10th grade at his Canadian boarding school, he came to me, uncertain.

"Mom, we have to choose our courses for next year, but I don't know what to pick."

"How many do you need?"

"Six to eight. Minimum six."

"What subject are you best at?"

"Math."

"Then start there. Pick all the math classes you can."

"That's three. I still need more…"

"What do you enjoy?"

"Honestly… I don't enjoy anything."

"Then choose the lightest options, something manageable while you figure things out."

He asked if he could take Art.

"Which is easier, watercolour or oil?"

"Oil," I said. "You can paint anything and call it abstract."

We laughed.

"Take English, that's five. You're already in Wood class this year, right? Take the Wood Sculpture next. Just build something bigger, give it a deep title, and you're done."

"You're a genius, Mom."

That day, Ghini registered for three math classes, English, Oil Painting, and Wood Sculpture.

He felt lighter and more in control.

This wasn't just about course selection.

It was a lesson in handling uncertainty.

When you don't know exactly what you want, the wisest choice is to keep moving, gently, wisely, until clarity finds you.

I told him:

"You don't have to figure everything out today.

Pick what is manageable.

And when your passion finds you, give it everything you have."

6. There Is No Real Happiness in Living a False Life

I once asked a successful friend, "Are you happy?"

He answered, "I don't know. I've never really lived the way I wanted."

That answer stayed with me for years.

It made me ask myself:

Are the things we teach our children, about success, morality, and effort, truly guiding them toward happiness?

Or are we simply training them to perform well while disconnecting from who they are?

Living authentically is the deepest form of honesty and the greatest act of courage.

If a child must wear a mask every day, to please others, to appear successful or happy,

While hiding their true identity, needs, and desires,

Then that life is no longer theirs.

I don't need my children to be officials, billionaires, or prodigies.

I just want them to live a peaceful life, doing work they love.

Because when you do what you love, even hard work feels like play.

Living true to yourself isn't selfish.

It's the only way to love others bsincerely and give to the world meaningfully.

7. Teach Your Child to Express Themselves with Honesty

Honesty isn't just about not telling lies.

It's about having the courage to express who you are, even when you're misunderstood.

As children grow, the pressure to fit in grows with them.

They may begin to hide parts of themselves to be accepted.

They shrink, soften, or silence their uniqueness.

I tell my children:

"You don't need to be the most impressive person.

Just don't betray yourself."

Honest self-expression doesn't mean saying everything out loud.

It means knowing your thoughts, feelings, and boundaries, and communicating them with care.

For example, if you no longer feel connected to a group of friends,

You don't have to pretend.

You can step back quietly and respectfully, while remaining honest with yourself.

I remind them often:

The truest honesty isn't always verbal.

It's the alignment between your inner world and how you live.

When you live as your real self, you naturally attract people who belong in your life,

Not because of who you pretend to be, but because of who you are.

8. When Your Child Falls – Don't Rush to Shield Them

Children cannot grow without facing difficulty.

And it's not the fall that defines them, but how they rise.

As a single mother, I've had the instinct to protect my children from every storm.

But I've learned, real love doesn't always mean protection.

Sometimes, love means trust.

It means stepping back so the child can learn to carry themselves.

"If one day you find yourself alone in the storm,

Remember, I never left.

But I won't hold the umbrella forever.

Because I believe you are strong enough to find your way."

9. Love Doesn't Mean Attachment

Before my children can love others, I teach them to love themselves.

Their body and soul are sacred.

They must be nourished, at peace, and fulfilled; only then can they give love that is true and lasting.

I don't ask them to sacrifice themselves endlessly.

I teach them to listen to their emotions, care for their health, protect their boundaries, and say "no" when needed.

Because those who cannot love themselves will one day give their hearts to the wrong people.

Once they understand self-love, I teach them to love their family, the people who stood by them from the beginning, who love without asking for anything in return.

Family is the first place we learn to give, to forgive, and to stay, even when life isn't perfect.

Only after these foundations are built can they begin to understand romantic love.

"True love is not about clinging to someone.

It's about holding on to yourself, while loving them."

Many mistake attachment for loyalty, or dependence for depth.

But real love is rooted in inner freedom.

It's about growing side by side, not losing yourself in someone else.

A child truly learns how to love when they know how to remain whole in love.

10. When Love Goes Wrong: Teach Them to Tell Real from Fake

I've loved the wrong person.

I've trusted promises that were never meant to be kept.

I thought that sacrifice would earn me love.

But real love doesn't need to be earned by pain.

I learned this the hard way.

That's why I want my daughters to understand it without having to cry first.

Even though they haven't spoken about dating yet, they're focused on school, so I still share my experience.

So one day, when they need it, they'll have this wisdom with them.

I don't teach them how to "keep" someone.

I teach them how to observe.

Because real love isn't in the words someone says or the gifts they give.

It's in how they treat you when you're weak, tired, or have nothing to offer.

"Don't judge by how they arrive, watch how they leave.

Don't listen to promises, look at their behavior when you have nothing left to give."

I teach my children to recognize quiet kindness:

The kind that asks for nothing.

The respect for boundaries.

The loyalty that stays even when you're not your best.

"Fake love always demands.

Real love walks beside you.

And only when you love yourself clearly will you be able to tell the difference."

11. Don't Give Your Heart to Someone Who Only Sees Your Value

In today's world, charm can mask selfishness.

Generosity can hide manipulation.

I teach my children:

Don't judge someone by their money.

Judge them by their character and work ethic.

I don't tell my daughters to marry someone poor, because poverty is rarely just bad luck.

It's often the result of laziness or poor choices.

A man with integrity, vision, and a strong will won't stay poor for long.

But a man who is still poor as an adult may be lacking either effort or direction.

"You don't need to choose someone rich.

Choose someone who stands on their own, and lives by principle."

And don't just look at how someone treats *you.*

Watch how they treat the cleaner. The waiter. The janitor.

"The way someone behaves at the dinner table, and how they speak to someone who serves them, that's how you know who they truly are."

Choosing a life partner should never be done blindly.

Ask yourself:

- Who will stand with you in a storm?
- And who will disappear the moment it gets hard?

12. A Good Man Doesn't Need to Be Wealthy

I've never told my son he has to become a "successful" man by society's standards.

But I've always taught him to be a decent man.

That has nothing to do with money.

You can be average, but you must be responsible, respectful, and considerate.

I start with the small things:

Teaching him to wash his socks and underwear,

Fold his blanket,

And never expect others to serve him for things he can do himself.

These habits are the roots of self-respect,

The building blocks of someone who is independent and thoughtful.

I teach him to thank servers, offer his seat to elders, apologize when wrong,

And treat everyone with dignity, especially those less fortunate.

"You don't have to be better than anyone, or richer,

But never live below the moral standard of a real man."

We talk about emotional regulation, keeping promises, and accepting responsibility.

Because no matter how wealthy someone is, if they break their word or avoid accountability, they are not trustworthy.

I don't need my son to be powerful. I need him to be reliable, Someone others feel safe with, someone who earns respect through his presence, not his position.

13. Marry Someone Truly Compatible, Not Just By Status

"When choosing a life partner, look for true compatibility.

Not in wealth or status, but in values, character, and worldview."

If you are kind, hardworking, and thoughtful, you won't thrive with someone who is lazy, selfish, or ungrateful.

If you grew up in a loving family, it will be hard to live with someone raised in fear, control, or emotional absence.

"Differences in background can be bridged.

But differences in thinking and character cannot be patched with love."

I don't tell my children to marry rich, but I do urge them to choose someone capable of caring for a family.

You cannot marry someone without ambition or skills and expect to carry everything alone in the name of love.

That's not love, that's a burden disguised as romance.

I guide them to look for real compatibility:

- Can you have deep conversations?
- Share responsibilities?
- Laugh in quiet moments?
- Navigate conflict without cruelty?

Marriage is not just between two people,

It's a merging of families and value systems.

Choose wisely.

Because if you choose wrong, it's not just the spouse who causes pain,

But the entire system that comes with them.

14. Teach Your Children to Be Responsible, Especially to Their Parents

I don't teach my children to repay me with money.

I teach them to care with sincerity, through everyday gestures.

"Filial piety doesn't mean expensive gifts.

It means not breaking your mother's heart."

I don't need grand celebrations.

What I cherish is:

- A message asking how I am
- A hug when I look down
- A glance of concern when I seem tired

When they were young, I taught them:

- Let me know when you arrive safely
- Say hello when you come home
- Notice if I'm quiet
- Apologize when you're wrong

Not because I'm weak,

But because I want them to see me as human.

Someone who deserves respect and tenderness.

I never pretended to be a perfect mother.

I let them see me cry, stumble, and rest, so they could understand that love means seeing one another fully.

When they see me as a person, they naturally feel responsible for me, not out of duty, but love.

I also teach my son to stay connected with his father, even though we don't live together.

To remember birthdays, call instead of remaining silent.

Because true respect for your roots stays, no matter where life takes you.

15. Freedom Means Living Without Debt

One of the first things I taught my children:

Don't live in debt.

Don't spend what you don't have.

Don't borrow today from tomorrow.

Because once you owe, whether money, love, or favors,

You are no longer free.

I've seen many young people post luxury online,

Wearing designer labels, eating lavish meals, and traveling the world.

But behind the screen, they are drowning in debt.

They fear being exposed.

And in the process, they lose their self-respect.

"Freedom isn't about how much you earn.

It's about not needing others to survive.

Don't spend borrowed money to maintain a life that isn't yours."

I teach my children to budget, even as students.

To separate needs from wants.

Not to shop out of emotion.

And most importantly, never buy love with money.

Because love bought with wealth will vanish the moment your wallet is empty.

I'm not against wealth.

But I believe:

Wealth with dependence is still poverty.

Simplicity with autonomy, that is, dignity.

"Self-respect begins when you stop borrowing others' trust.

And freedom begins when you owe nothing to anyone, including yourself."

CHAPTER IV
FALLING DOWN TO LEARN TO STAND

1. When Your Child Falls, Don't Rush to Lift Them

A parent's instinct is to protect, especially when a child gets a bad grade, is teased, or stumbles in life. But in those moments, what children need most is not rescue, but a parent's quiet belief that they can rise on their own.

Developmental psychology shows that between ages six and twelve, children begin forming a sense of personal competence, the belief, "I can do this."

If parents over-intervene, children become dependent and lose trust in their own abilities.

What parents can do:

- When your child struggles, ask: "Would you like me to watch while you try, or do you want help?"

- After a setback, avoid saying: "Never mind, I'll do it next time." Instead, ask: "What could you try differently next time?"
- Share your own stories of failure and how you moved past them.

I'll never forget the moment I instinctively pushed my daughter away when she threw up. My reaction didn't match my heart, and I regretted it deeply. That painful memory taught me that holding a child close is not only instinct, it's also a choice that must be practiced.

2. Help Children Learn from Failure, Not Fear It

Fear of failure is often rooted in fear of rejection, what psychologists call the fear of shame. Children become afraid of making mistakes when those mistakes are met with punishment, mockery, or comparison.

Over time, this leads them to believe: "If I fail, I'm not good enough." They stop taking risks, avoid challenges, and struggle with creativity.

What parents can do:

- Ask: "What did you learn from this?" instead of "Why did you do so badly?"
- Acknowledge effort: "You worked hard. It didn't go as planned, but I'm proud that you didn't give up."
- Encourage reflection: "If you could do it again, what would you do differently?"

You don't need to be a psychologist to help your child. Just listening calmly and consistently can help them view failure as part of growth, not something to fear.

3. True Growth Comes from Taking Responsibility

Children between the ages of six and nine begin to understand cause and effect and develop a sense of accountability. They gain self-respect by completing tasks and owning their actions.

If parents always blame teachers, friends, or circumstances, children may learn to shift blame instead of learning from mistakes.

What parents can do:

- Ask: "What do you think you could do better next time?" rather than blaming others.
- Normalize mistake-making by sharing your own stories.
- Praise honesty and accountability, even before the problem is solved.

Responsibility is the foundation of freedom. Only when children understand where they went wrong can they begin to choose more wisely in the future.

4. Give Your Child the Right to Be Wrong

No child grows up whole without making mistakes. Falling and still feeling loved is only possible in an environment rooted in safety and respect.

When children are allowed to make choices and experience failure within safe boundaries, they begin to develop self-correction, resilience, and independence.

What parents can do:

- Allow small decisions, like what to wear or what activity to try.

- If a decision leads to a mistake, stay nearby, but let them navigate the consequences unless they ask for help.
- Talk through the experience afterwards: "Why did you choose that? What did you learn?"

Respect doesn't mean always agreeing. It means creating space for your child to learn through experience.

5. Crying Isn't Weakness: Teach Children to Name Emotions

In emotional psychology, naming feelings is essential for emotional regulation. Children who are unable to express sadness or anger often develop unhealthy coping behaviors—tantrums, withdrawal, or even self-harm.

But when children are taught that emotions are natural and safe to express, they grow up with greater self-compassion.

What parents can do:

- Ask questions that encourage emotional reflection: "What made you happy today?" or "Was there anything that made you feel sad?"

- When your child cries, avoid saying, "Stop crying." Instead, say, "I see you're upset. Would you like a hug?"
- Encourage writing or drawing as tools for processing emotions.

A child who can name and understand their feelings is more likely to show empathy, and this emotional intelligence is far more valuable than any academic score.

6. Help Your Child Stop Fearing Judgment

Around age eight, children become more aware of how others see them. If they are repeatedly labeled or criticized, they may begin to hide their true selves.

Some children withdraw. Others become people-pleasers, constantly chasing approval at the expense of authenticity.

What parents can do:

- Avoid correcting or criticizing your child in front of others. Private, respectful correction is more effective.

- Focus on effort, not perfection. Ask, "Did you do your best?" rather than, "Why didn't you get a perfect score?"
- Share your own stories of being misjudged and how you stayed true to yourself.

When a child knows their value doesn't depend on approval, they become more confident in trying, failing, and staying true to themselves.

7. Parents Are Not Perfect, and Neither Are Children

Trying to be the perfect parent can cast a heavy shadow. But children don't need flawless role models. They need human ones.

They need parents who can apologize, who admit when they're wrong, who keep learning and growing, just like they are.

What parents can do:

- Say sorry when you lose patience or make a mistake: "I'm sorry I raised my voice yesterday. I'll do better next time."

- Show your own growth: "I read something today that helped me understand your feelings more."
- Teach that imperfection is not failure. It's a chance to try again.

Your child's growth isn't defined by success. It's reflected in the courage to be themselves, openly, imperfectly, and without fear.

CHAPTER V
PARENTING WITH WISDOM AND LOVE

No one teaches us how to be parents.

We enter this sacred role with inexperience, guided by instinct or repeating what we learned from our own parents, whether those lessons were helpful or not.

However, every child is a unique soul.

To truly support them, parents must also be willing to grow, learn, and heal.

Love is the foundation.

But without wisdom, love can turn into control, blind sacrifice, or emotional burden.

Wise parenting means knowing:

- When to teach and when to listen
- When to guide and when to let go
- When to be firm and when to be gentle
- When to walk beside and when to step back

Raising a child is not only about their development.

It is a journey of transformation for us as parents as well.

1. Parenting Is Not Sacrifice. It Is Growing Alongside Your Child

People often call me a brave mother.

They say I "sacrificed my youth" for my children.

It sounds noble. But when we frame parenting as sacrifice, we risk sending the wrong message and draining ourselves.

Parents who feel they "gave up everything" often become tired and resentful.

Even without saying it out loud, they may pass on guilt:

"Because of you, I lost so much."

Children raised in that energy may feel obligated to succeed, not for themselves,

But to repay a debt they never agreed to.

Healthy love is rooted in freedom and mutual respect.

Children learn self-love and self-respect by watching parents who live with peace and fulfillment, not exhaustion or regret.

How parents can begin:

- Write down five things you've learned through being a parent
- Set aside time each week to read, walk, or meet a friend
- Say honestly to your child, "Mom needs a break today. Let's lie down and listen to music together."

2. Heal Yourself Before Trying to Heal Your Child

Many parents hurt their children unintentionally. They carry wounds from their own childhood that were never addressed.

A mother who was constantly criticized may struggle with patience.

A father who was taught to suppress emotions may scold his son for crying.

Children learn more from our actions than our words.

Our inner peace is the soil where their emotional security grows.

How parents can begin:

- When you feel triggered, pause and ask, "Is this coming from my child or my own past?"
- Keep a journal or practice mindfulness.
- Read books on healing your inner child, or seek professional support if needed

3. Build Inner Strength Instead of Controlling Your Child

When a child is overly controlled, they may become overly obedient and lose their voice,

Or they may become rebellious in an effort to reclaim power.

Neither outcome is healthy.

Children need age-appropriate autonomy.

Only when trusted can they grow into confident and responsible people.

How parents can begin:

- Let your child help with decisions that affect them, such as choosing a class or decorating their room
- Assign simple tasks like folding clothes, watering plants, or wiping the table
- When mistakes happen, ask, "What did you learn?" instead of, "Why were you careless?"

4. Teach with Words, Raise with Action

Children learn by watching.

Words that are not backed by actions lose meaning.

When parents say one thing but live another, children either become skeptical or mirror those contradictions.

Trust and character grow from example, not lectures.

How parents can begin:

- Apologize when you're wrong
- Say thank you when your child helps

- Show kindness to everyone, especially those who serve or are vulnerable

These small actions become your child's internal compass.

5. Love Doesn't Mean Doing Everything. It Means Empowering

Many parents do everything for their children, packing bags, cleaning, choosing clothes, thinking it shows love.

But overdoing it can take away a child's chance to learn and believe in themselves.

True love means helping a child build their own skills,

So they can stand tall with confidence.

How parents can begin:

- Teach basic self-care starting at age four
- When they struggle with homework, ask, "What part do you find most challenging?" rather than doing it for them.

- Let them choose weekend activities or what to wear, so they feel included and capable.

6. Teach Love Through Example, Not Orders

Love cannot be forced. It grows when modeled.

Children learn how to love by watching how we treat others.

They observe how we show up, how we help without being asked, how we stay through difficulty.

Since middle school, I have taken my children every summer to visit orphanages and centers for children with disabilities, places I had supported for years.

I didn't want to simply talk about compassion.

I wanted them to feel it, by holding babies with no parents, by feeding children who could not feed themselves, by seeing suffering not as something to avoid but something to answer with kindness.

I hoped these moments would plant seeds of empathy in their hearts.

Over time, they did more than that.

One day, my twin daughters, Lu and Li, in their second year at the University of Toronto, said to me,

"Mom, from now on, don't worry about us. We'll work part-time to pay for our tuition and rent. You focus on helping Ghini."

For three years, I only paid for my son's schooling.

My daughters managed their own expenses while studying one of Canada's toughest programs.

Then, in 2024, Ghini graduated from high school and was accepted into the same university. Lu and Li said,

"Since we all go to the same school now, let Ghini live with us. We'll cover the rent and help raise him."

I told them, "Only if you don't overwork yourselves. School is still the priority. If you need anything, come to me."

What moved me most wasn't just their sense of responsibility.

I hadn't expected the thoughtfulness.

One evening, Ghini showed me his new room. It had a large window, a balcony with a view, and good space.

I asked, "Why do you have the biggest room?"

He answered, "Lu chose the smallest one so I could study more comfortably."

This was the same sister who worked the hardest and carried the greatest financial load.

Yet she quietly chose the smallest space so her younger brother could have the comfort she didn't.

That isn't just kindness.

That is maturity, sacrifice, and real, unconditional love.

As a mother, I was overwhelmed.

Not just because all three children made it to one of Canada's most prestigious universities—

But because they had become generous, compassionate human beings.

In that moment, all the years of effort felt worthwhile.

I was no longer raising children.

I was watching them raise each other.

CHAPTER VI
CHOOSING A LIFE WORTH LIVING

1. A Child Is to Love, Not to Possess

All parents love their children.

But love is not always expressed in the right way.

Some try to control their children, thinking it's for their own good.

Others project their own unfulfilled dreams onto them,

Expecting them to succeed where they did not.

But your child is not your clone.

They are a free soul, here to live their own truth.

"You are not here to bring glory to your parents.

You are not here to continue a bloodline.

You are here to love and be loved, freely and fully."

Don't live to meet expectations.

Live by your values.

Be true to who you are.

2. Character Is More Precious Than Success

Society often praises wealth and fame.

But I hope you learn to admire something deeper:

Kindness, integrity, gratitude, and compassion.

You don't have to be the best.

But always be decent.

You don't have to earn the most.

But never cheat to get ahead.

A person of strong character will not sell their soul for profit.

They will not stay silent when their voice is needed.

"One day, you will understand:

Living clean and upright is the most beautiful gift I've given you."

3. Don't Let Love Become a Debt

Real love does not demand repayment.

It never makes you feel like you owe anything.

Be cautious of relationships where you feel the need to "earn" love.

Those who truly care will never ask you to trade your freedom for affection,

Or abandon your truth to keep them happy.

Love should feel like growth, not loss.

It should bring light, not weight.

Love is growing together, not fading away to please someone else.

4. Compatibility Lies in Character, Not Wealth

"Don't marry for possessions. Look at their spirit.

Don't marry for appearance. Choose character and empathy."

True compatibility isn't about matching social status.

It's about aligning in values, culture, and worldview.

Good people are drawn to good people.

The kind-hearted belong with the responsible.

The patient matches well with the gentle.

If you want lasting joy,

Choose someone capable of kindness, not just in good times,

But especially when life becomes hard.

5. Choose Work That Makes You Proud, Not Others Happy

Don't choose a career for status, money, or to please your parents.

Choose something where you can be yourself, no pretending, no pressure.

Success isn't in job titles.

It's in waking up every morning knowing your work has meaning.

Find a path worth walking,

Even if no one applauds.

Even if it takes longer to build.

The life that feels right is better than the one that only looks right.

6. A Debt-Free Life Is Light and Noble

Life will always bring its struggles.

But live within your means.

Don't borrow to impress others.

Don't spend to keep up appearances.

The person who owes nothing is the freest.

Free from the weight of debt.

Free from the burden of guilt.

Free from the pressure to pretend.

No debt of money.

No debt of favors.

No debt of trust.

I chose to live this way, and I hope you do too.

Live with truth.

Live with independence.

And carry no burden that takes you away from yourself.

CONCLUSION

(For the parents who made it to the final page)

Every parent hopes their child will grow into a good person. But we often forget that children don't grow through lessons alone. They grow by watching how we live. The way we speak, the way we respond, the way we love—these are the true teachings that shape their hearts.

I didn't write this book to instruct. I wrote it to reflect. To share what I've lived, the mistakes I've made, and the ways I've tried to make them right. I wrote it to honour the journey of watching my three children grow through loneliness, effort, love, and many tearful nights.

Some of the most powerful lessons came only after I had already caused pain. Some of my mistakes were forgiven by my children before I could even find the words to say sorry. That grace, that quiet strength in them, is what inspired me to grow.

This book is a promise I made to myself. A promise to mother with more awareness, more compassion, and fewer regrets each day. I know I cannot be perfect. But I can choose to be present. I can choose to grow with them.

If you are a parent, I invite you to begin with yourself. You don't need to have all the answers. You only need to love enough, understand enough, and be brave enough to walk this path with your child.

Raising a child is a journey. But raising yourself in order to raise your child is the deepest journey of all.

Thank you for walking with me to the very last page.

— **Lương Hoàng Anh**

www.ingramcontent.com/pod-product-compliance
Lightning Source LLC
Chambersburg PA
CBHW041452010526
44107CB00013B/1017